Philosophy and the Idea of Communism

T0087484

Philosophy and the Idea of Communism

Alain Badiou in conversation with
Peter Engelmann

Translated by Susan Spitzer

polity

First published in German as *Philosophie und die Idee des Kommunismus*
© Passagen Verlag GmbH, 2013

This English edition © Polity Press, 2015

Polity Press
65 Bridge Street
Cambridge CB2 1UR, UK

Polity Press
350 Main Street
Malden, MA 02148, USA

ISBN-13: 978-0-7456-8835-0 (hardback)
ISBN-13: 978-0-7456-8836-7 (paperback)

A catalogue record for this book is available from the British Library.

Library of Congress Cataloging-in-Publication Data

Badiou, Alain.
[Philosophie und die Idee des Kommunismus. English]
Philosophy and the idea of communism : Alain Badiou in conversation with Peter
Engelmann / Alain Badiou, Peter Engelmann. -- English edition.
pages cm
Includes bibliographical references.
ISBN 978-0-7456-8835-0 (hardback) -- ISBN 978-0-7456-8836-7 (pbk.)
1. Philosophers--France--Interviews. 2. Communism. 3. Political science--Philosophy.
I. Engelmann, Peter, interviewer. II. Title.
B2430.B274A5 2015
355.4'11--dc23

2014043391

Typeset in 12.5 on 15 pt Adobe Garamond by
Servis Filmsetting Ltd, Stockport, Cheshire
Printed and bound in the UK by Clays Ltd., St. Ives PLC

For further information on Polity, visit our website: politybooks.com

23 March 2012

Peter Engelmann Before we turn to the specific topic of our discussion, "the Idea of communism" in your philosophical work, I'd like to contextualize these questions in terms of both philosophy and politics. In your philosophy you develop a concept of the subject different from that of capitalist society, which views the subject reductively as a consumer and an economic competitor. The concept of the subject has a long history in philosophy, and in France there has been, as well, a theory of the death of the subject. What I'm interested in is how your concept of the subject has been inscribed in the French philosophical context since the 1960s to 1970s.

Alain Badiou   I'd like to make two comments about this. First of all, my first great philosophical influence was Sartre, in the 1950s. During all my early years of studying philosophy I considered the category of the subject to be fundamental, and it was, in particular in the form of the free consciousness, as Sartre was developing it at the time. I can therefore say that, philosophically, I come from, or come out of, a philosophy dominated by the theory of the subject, with a phenomenological vocabulary. So it was the subject in Sartre's sense, but also in Merleau-Ponty's sense, or even in Husserl's sense. Starting in the late 1950s, when I arrived at the École Normale, met Althusser, read Derrida's first books, and encountered Lacan's teaching, I became involved in what was called structuralism at the time, that is, a philosophy in which the subject is problematic. In Althusser's view, the subject was an ideological concept, a bourgeois concept. In the view of Lévi-Strauss and the structuralist tradition, it was structures that mattered, and, in the Heideggerian tradition, the subject was a concept from metaphysics that needed to be deconstructed. So I came into contact with all these things at that time, but with a sort of instinctive resistance that had a philosophical origin – the teaching of Sartre and of the great phenomenology of the period – as well as more personal or practical roots, which were that I couldn't see how you could do without the category of the subject in politics.

PE Why wasn't it possible to give up the subject in politics?

AB In politics in particular, because it was very clear to me that politics was a matter of orientation, action, decisions, and principles, a matter that demanded a subject or a subjective dimension. I observed, moreover, that the attempt to reduce politics – and Marxism – to a purely objective, purely structural, context, without the figure of a subject, led to nothing but a sort of pure economism, in which it wasn't even clear what political action properly speaking, as decisive, voluntary, and constructive action, was. For all these reasons, I got involved in structuralism nonetheless, along with my friends at the time, but with the idea that it ought to be possible to reconcile the teachings of structuralism and/ or deconstruction with a renewal of the concept of the subject, by transforming and retaining the category of the subject. Ultimately, I think the most important teaching for me back then was Lacan's, because Lacan was someone who, on the one hand, attached great importance to structures and particularly to the structures of language – the unconscious is structured like a language, etc. – but who, on the other hand, as heir to the psychoanalytic tradition, naturally retained the category of the subject. He not only retained it but even transformed it, making it into something absolutely central. So I regarded this teaching as a chance to find a way in which some of the lessons of speculative modernity could be accepted while at the same time the category of the subject could still be retained, in exchange, of course, for an important transformation of that theory. I think this has remained my project to this day.

PE I have long wondered how you define your position in this connection. You said that it was impossible to act without the concept of the subject, particularly with regard to politics. But I'd like to go back to philosophy. You alluded to some philosophers who developed a critique of the concept of the subject, but then you switched abruptly to politics.

AB No, I simply gave politics as *one* example of a field of creativity and activity in which the whole problem is precisely the construction of a subject.

PE Would you agree if I said that a concept of the subject is needed in every field of human endeavor?

AB We'd have to make a detour, in that case, because the concept of the subject in my work is closely linked to two other concepts – that of event and that of truth. A subject is always a subject of truth. It is always the subject for or in a process of constructing a truth. My way of critiquing the metaphysical concept of the subject is to say that the subject is a creation or a construction, and that it's not a given. What is given is in the form of the individual, for example. But "individual" and "subject" are not one and the same for me. Ultimately, they're even in a completely fundamental opposition to each other, even though individuals are always called to become subjects or to be incorporated into a subject. It's a summons, not a constant, natural movement. And this summons occurs via a real process, which might be political but might also be something else. It might be a political process, or an artistic process, or an amorous process. In all these cases there is a subjective summons.

PE Would you agree that a critique of the concept of the subject is warranted, but, at the same time, a critique of the individual isn't possible, since the individual is a given?

AB Absolutely.

PE I think that's very important because it helps solve some of the problems with deconstruction.

AB I think the important thing, as far as the critique of the concept of the subject is concerned, is to understand that it's a critique targeting a particular philosophical construction, which has a history. I accept the idea that the concept of the subject, as it has been construed from Descartes to Sartre, is in some respects a metaphysical concept or construction. When I say I'm reviving the category of the subject, it's in a completely different context. I naturally agree that there's a sort of fusion of individual and subject in the metaphysical tradition. Take the subject of the Cartesian *cogito*, for example: it's a construction that ultimately refers to an individual experience. Even Sartrean consciousness is an individual consciousness. Sartre himself identified the individual in terms of his/her subjective figure, that is, on the basis of his/her conscious figure. So what I retain from the deconstruction of the metaphysical category of the subject is that the ubiquitous construction tacking the subject onto the individual has to be dismantled. On the one hand, there will be the subjective construction linked to truth procedures, and, on the other, as its irreducible support, the individual, which I sometimes also call the "human animal" and is a given, a given I'd simply call natural or, in other words, ordinary. Individuals exist in the figure of the world, but it's not because they exist that they should be called subjects.

PE If I understand correctly, your last comment suggests that the individual, as an existing individual, is not deconstructible. But we also know, for example, that Hegel begins *The Phenomenology of Spirit* with the demonstration that there is no here and now apart from language. This is the exact opposite position, on the basis of which he constructs his metaphysical system. Hegel's system assumes that the given is right from the start a given of language. He holds that the here and now is only accessible to us in and through language, and he reconstructs the world through the system of philosophical science. But the given thereby loses its immediacy. Thus, the individual is no longer the felt or willed individual but is always already linguistic. This poses a real problem for philosophical discourse but also for the representation of the "true" interests of "real" individuals. I myself have always instinctively resisted the dethroning of the individual or stressed the fact that there is indeed an undeconstructible or inescapable individuality, and in my critique of Hegel I've always been on the individual's side against the domination by the language process. But I can also see the criticism that could be directed at me, and I direct it at myself as well: In light of the Hegelian critique, how can one insist on the immediacy

8

of the individual? What does this imply now for philosophical resistance? Is there a philosophical argument that can be opposed to that resistance?

AB I agree with pointing out the individual's instinctive resistance to deconstruction, but only provided that it's clearly understood that this individual is nothing but a "there is." S/he is the "there is" of humanity as animality, nothing more. So the individual as such is irreducible, but that doesn't give him/her any particular value other than that of his/her life. In other words, I agree with the idea of the irreducibility of the individual, but only on condition that the individual's value is not opposed to the metaphysical subject's value, as if they were on a par with each other. I don't, for example, agree with Kierkegaard's critique of Hegel. Kierkegaard says the individual's life is ultimately irreducible. I agree with that, but not so as to prepare the ground, as is the case with Kierkegaard, for a sanctification of the individual in an ultimately religious figure. In other words, human life, in its irreducibility, is nothing but the life of human animality as such. So you could say that it's the irreducibility of a body, of a living body. A living body is in effect irreducible; it's not deconstructible.

PE Of course, you can't emphasize the individual's irreducibility and then turn around and give him/her additional value.

AB That's the whole point. That's why I said that Kierkegaard's strategy was to deconstruct the Hegelian system in order to bring out the individual's subjective irreducibility, but ultimately in a theological context, a religious context. In my view, there's nothing in the individual other than the existing animality, the principle of life. Life is individuated; it presents itself in a context of both species and individuation, and for that reason it is not deconstructible. But the fact that it's not deconstructible doesn't give it any value other than that of bare life. Then, the question as to what value bare life has is something that will only take on its meaning from the perspective of a subjectivated truth.

PE Don't we have to use another approach if we want to add values to that existing individuality?

AB   No, not exactly. It's only from the perspective of the possible emergence of the category of the subject that the question of the individual's value even arises, because the individual, as such, constitutes no value other than the perseverance of his/her life. "To strive to persevere in being," as Spinoza said.

PE   So the concept of the subject is the medium through which all values are thought?

AB   Yes, absolutely. All valorizations take place within the subject. But that shouldn't be confused with the idea that the individual, all on his/her own, as in Hegel, triggers the process that will eventually arrive at the Absolute. And if there's nothing but the perseverance of life, the individual doesn't constitute any space of valorization, nor does s/he by him/herself set the subjective process going. Something else is required, which I call an event.

PE   In Hegel, the starting point of phenomenology is something from which we have to free ourselves.

AB That's because, in Hegel, there's the work of negativity, so individuality, insofar as it is worked from within as negativity, tends to overcome itself.

PE But that's just it: it's subjectivity, not individuality...

AB As Hegel says, the Absolute is with us right from the start. Subjectivity is in the individual. There's already the work of negativity that will arrange it in the successive figures of consciousness, because the Absolute is at work in individuality. That's the whole problem. *I* don't think there's any Absolute at work in individuality.

PE That's my view, too. That's where I see a problem in Hegel.

AB The individual is abandoned by the Absolute, that's all. I nonetheless retain the category of absoluteness, but in a different respect: in terms of the fact that the truths a particular subject is capable of – the truths constructed by the subjective figure that may emerge, that are a possibility – can be absolutes in a way, because they're universal and aren't relative to the context in which they're produced. In fact, I think that speaking about truth without speaking about the Absolute is meaningless. If truths are relative, they are actually indistinguishable from opinions.

I note in passing that the critique of the Hegelian Absolute as an integral part of the work of negativity – which will eventually raise individuality to subjectivity and subjectivity to the figure of consciousness, and will culminate in philosophical and dialectical consciousness, etc. – I note that the critique of this initial Absolute (and final Absolute, too, moreover, since what's at the end is also what's at the beginning) doesn't mean for me that nothing can be said to be absolute. "Absolute" must be taken in its most basic sense, namely, what is not relative, what is universal, what is not dependent and is not connected in an essential way to the conditions of its construction.

PE Do you really believe that?

AB That there's an absolute of that sort? Of course I do, absolutely. And, for me, mathematical, scientific, artistic, amorous, and political truths exist with an absolute meaning or value.

PE And how is that absolute truth related to human finitude?

AB Human beings are neither finite nor infinite as such. They have access to the infinite, obviously. We are able to think the infinite in a variety of ways.

PE Is there a spirit, as in Hegel, that is not subject to thought, absolute spirit?

AB There's no such thing as absolute spirit. The subjective construction of a truth is related to the infinite, simply because the infinite is the real. The real is infinite; it is not finite. So if you have a truth, it must touch the infinity of the real. If you don't have a truth that touches the real, you don't have a framework for producing this truth and thinking it at the same time. So I argue that human thought itself is potentially in the element of the infinite. This is not a problem for me, and in my next book I intend to show that it's the finite that's problematic.

PE How is the finite problematic for you?

AB What this means is that everything is infinite. The real is infinite, and truths, insofar as they touch the real, are related to the infinite. The question of finitude is one in which, in a sense, the finite is always an outcome. It's the infinite that's the mode of being of everything that is, and the finite, on the contrary, in the form of the work of art, for example, is a finite sampling of the infinite. It's the finite that's a product and the infinite that, on the contrary, is the given. When it comes to this issue, the tradition, which has always made finitude self-evident and the infinite something transcendent or inaccessible, must be completely reversed. I think it's the exact opposite. The issue isn't the infinite; the issue is the most basic "there is." Then, how thought makes it way, or how something can be created, an idea that touches the infinite, is a different, rather complicated problem. But it's there that subjectivity emerges. You could also say, if you like, that what we call a "subject" is when individuals, or one individual, are summoned to the reality of the infinite. That's what a subject is. And it is summoned to the reality of the infinite by singular events that cannot be inferred from individuality – there is no natural dialectic – but that will gradually create the subjective ability to have access to the infinity of the real and to forge a path in it, a vision that will have universal significance and, in that sense, can be termed absolute. That's what the question of the absolute is. The details are pretty complicated, but the original intuitions are simple enough. The basic gesture as regards this issue is to reverse the usual scheme whereby it's infinity that is transcendentally inaccessible and finitude that is the inevitable human destiny. There are already a few hints of this sort of reversal in Descartes, who, in several of his texts, says that the infinite is actually simpler than the finite. This was an intuition he had already expressed. What's more, in the *Meditations*, it's clear that the proof that the real exists assumes that the infinite is required, since it's only through the proof of God's existence that it can be ensured that there is anything real. I agree with this very strong intuition of Descartes' that all access to the real, all real certainty, involves the mediation of the infinite. Thus, there is an organic relationship between the infinity of being, the access to this infinity of being, the various different truth procedures, and the fact that the subject is the instigator of all this, inasmuch as it summons the individual to this action or process. As for the individual, s/he is neither finite nor infinite, strictly speaking, because s/he is finite from an external descriptive point of view – there is death, the body's limits, anything you like – but, as s/he is also capable of the infinite, his/her finitude cannot be said to be irreducible. S/he is capable of having access to the infinite, s/he is capable of touching the infinity of the real, s/he is capable of operating within it, and s/he is also capable of creating, out of this infinity, a finite with universal value, a finitude with universal value. The most classic examples of this are the work of art, or a political revolution, or a new scientific fact. There are many different examples. In all these cases, we encounter that subjective production that touches the infinity of the real.

PE   So the individual becomes a subject when s/he touches the infinite?

AB   Yes, when s/he touches the real infinite. But I'm leery of the phrase "the individual becomes a subject." I prefer to say: "the individual becomes incorporated into a subject," because it's not always, and most of the time it's not even, an individual who becomes a subject. The political subject, for example, is a collective subject, not an individual. Likewise, one might wonder what the artistic subject is. There has been endless speculation about genius all throughout history. In fact, it's somewhere in between the individual and the collective, because there are always schools, groups, and collective creations as well, in which creative subjectivity is ultimately situated. This is also very true of the sciences, where there is always a scientific community that serves, in the final analysis, as a validation of what a given scientist has discovered. I think it's more accurate to say that the individual – with all his/her receptivity, with his/her body, his/her thought, what s/he does, his/her social being, the language s/he speaks – is incorporated into the subjective process. The latter is always a unique process and never covers the whole life of the individual because the aspect of the individual that's incorporated into the subjective process is itself a unique aspect, a sample, so to speak, of the individual. Furthermore, the individual has to go on eating and nourishing his/her body, become ill, and ultimately die. All those things will continue, but the capacity to touch the infinite will have nonetheless been experienced through the individual's partial – sometimes transient, sometimes more permanent – incorporation into a procedure where the real infinite is touched. This means we could say: every individual can participate in the absolute. I'm not saying that every individual *becomes* absolute – because that would be like saying there was an absolute subject taking in all individuals – but s/he can *participate in* the absolute. This is a possibility that's ultimately open to every individual but that involves an element of chance.

PE And that subject, the individual who touches the infinite, isn't targeted by deconstruction, Lacan's critique?

AB I don't think so, because it's absolutely not subjectivity in the sense of the metaphysical or Cartesian subject or even Sartrean consciousness that's involved. It's a sort of partial possibility, which is immanent in the individual as a partial possibility and, in addition, needs an outside intervention in order to happen. That is the question of the event, i.e., the idea that something must happen in the human animal's life that opens this possibility to him/her. If you assume that that possibility can develop all by itself, you become a Hegelian again. So there's an element of chance. It is, after all, the element of limitation that I'm describing in this process, which every individual is potentially capable of. And there's a summons, the most striking example of which is the amorous encounter. You meet someone – often by chance – and even though something of the infiniteness of life may well be touched in love, chance was still necessary for the encounter to have happened. Likewise, in politics, we know very well – to take the recent example of the great uprisings in the Arab world – that, for most of the people involved, only a few days before they had no idea they had the ability to do such a thing. And there's no doubt that, at that moment, they had the feeling of touching the infinite. You only have to think about the statements they made, even if they were very basic statements, such as: "We are Egypt." What all this really means is: we touched something that surpassed us. That fact remains irreversible and absolute. Even if the whole affair didn't lead to an absolute change in terms of subjective creation, it existed for all time. Naturally, this had nothing to do with the self-development of the individual who transcends the here and now. No, it was an impetus. Deleuze said that we always think in response to an outside impetus – in his work, it was the category of the outside – and I think he was right. In my work, it's developed to some extent in the category of the figure of the event, but it's the same idea. It's the anti-Hegelian idea that, in order for the subjective elevation of the individual to really occur, something must come from outside.

PE   In Hegel, there's no such "outside."

AB   No, and Hegel even tries to put everything "inside."

PE   You show very clearly where the problem lies in Hegel. Does something change with Nietzsche and his image of the death of God?

AB   Nietzsche's distinctive contribution should not be underestimated. Essentially, I think his contribution comes down to asking: "What might man's or humanity's creative power be if God doesn't exist, if the God of Christianity and, more specifically, the redeeming God of Christianity, doesn't exist? If our human nature hasn't been redeemed by God, if it's reduced to itself, what is it capable of?" In a way, this is the question that concerns me, too, and so I understand Nietzsche very well when it comes to this issue. In fact, we can turn to Dostoyevsky, who thought that if God was dead, everything was permitted. But the contemporary mind-set is actually a lot more like: "If God is dead, nothing is permitted." What's more, if God is dead, we aren't capable of anything; we have to be content with what there is. I think there's actually a sort of negative atheism holding sway over Western societies, which amounts to saying that we will in fact do without God, but, by the same token, we'll do without everything that went along with Him: the absolute; subjective salvation; the capacity to do and desire the good; mysticism. All those things will disappear, and, ultimately, without God, the point is just to live as comfortably as possible. There is, moreover, a possible answer to Nietzsche's question, an answer he himself didn't provide, which is: "If God is dead, let's stop longing for the absolute." God is dead; the absolute has no purpose; there are no truths; there are only opinions. The pursuit of material happiness is humanity's sole *raison d'être*, so let's just be content with what we have. That is really what the dominant thinking is today. It's actually the nihilistic lesson drawn from the hypothesis. That's why, when Dostoyevsky says "If God is dead, everything is permitted," in a way, that "everything" is very small. Everything is permitted, but everything's not a whole lot. Some interpretations of the death of God are actually a way of reducing human possibilities to the pleasantest material survival possible, period. But that wasn't Nietzsche's answer.

PE Does that interpretation imply that we're dealing with a restriction of human possibilities, and human capabilities, too, in the sphere of ethics, work, and social life?

AB Absolutely. Human beings are declared to be capable of very little. For example, the idea of committing oneself completely to something is absurd – sacrifice is a horrible idea, and so on. It's very clear that the real problem raised by

Dostoevsky's dictum is: "What is 'everything'?" Indeed, you realize that it's practically nothing; it's only the human animal's perseverance in life. That's it. You have to make do with that. Nietzsche's greatness, I believe, is not to have adopted this nihilistic way at all, even though he clearly saw that there was a possibility of nihilism. He tried to combat that nihilism by saying that, in spite of everything, Man is capable of overcoming Man. That's what the Overman is all about. The Overman can doubtless be understood in the fascistic way as a kind of nationalistic heroism. But it can also be understood as something positive.

PE How can it be understood as something positive? How do you see the positive in the Overman?

AB Yes, the Overman can mean that, under the conditions of the death of God, Man can go beyond himself, i.e., maintain his capacity, his openness, and so on. I think there's still a tendency in Nietzsche – I don't know what to call it – a "biological" tendency, after all. "Biological" because it consists in trying to extract from life itself, from the human animal's life, something that's in the regime of power. This is a current of thought that has continued up to Deleuze today, by way of Bergson. In my view, the individual can be diverted from his/her purely animal existence by an outside event that will propel him/her in the direction of a truth procedure, and this will allow him/her to touch the infinity of being. By contrast, in Nietzsche's view, as in Deleuze's, human beings can find an opportunity for creativity in the force of animal life itself. This is the idea that life is ultimately always more powerful than individuation, that it is more powerful than the individual, that the living individual possesses, in life, something more powerful than him/herself. I don't believe any such thing; I think this is, oddly enough, a biologized Hegelianism, namely that the individual possesses the absolute within him/herself, in the figure of the absolute of life. I don't believe that the force of life can be summoned as an immanent capacity for overcoming individuality. I've always found that this Nietzschean or Deleuzian view of things, which regards itself as the exact opposite of Hegel, wasn't as opposite to him as all that, because, when all is said and done, it, too, meant that the absolute is with us.

It's just that the absolute isn't spirit, as in Hegel; it's life itself.

PE Is it a matter of a substitution, then?

AB Yes, of spirit by life. It's biological. And it is what will lead to the Overman – in any case, that's my final verdict on Nietzsche. The original question was a very compelling one, in my opinion. The temptation to seek a solution in the life force seems misguided to me, though, because, in my view, the life force is actually utterly blind. It's not a force that truly orients one toward anything. It's a force that is the force of its own self-perpetuation, but at the level of its immanent capacity.

PE What about Marx? Marx was a philosopher. He was Hegelian. There was that thesis of Feuerbach's that turned the Hegelian dialectic on its head. Is that a case of switching from one principle to another, as you said a moment ago about Nietzsche?

AB That temptation can be found in Marx, of course. It was a temptation that I'd say was typical of the nineteenth century, moreover, and can also be found – this betokens a certain interpretation of Darwin – in some of the interpretations that were given of Freud and psychoanalysis. There was a certain positivistic, nineteenth-century hopefulness in all these major writers. But what I want to say about Marx is that there are actually three different Marxes, three things that don't mesh altogether seamlessly in him. There's the legacy of Hegelian philosophy, the dialectic, and this dialectic is mainly conceived of as an objective one, that is, as a development of contradictions. This is the Marx who constructed a philosophy of history, actually, an expansive vision of the movement of history.

PE Is Marx's history of philosophy actually Hegel's?

AB Absolutely. There's a substitution of materialism for the Hegelian vision of the history of philosophy, which is marked by a considerable element of necessity. The successive stages follow on from one another in a necessary way: there's the transition from feudalism to capitalism and, prior to that, the transition from slavery to feudalism. This is the Marx I'd call a philosopher of history.

PE   Right, he uses Hegelian logic.

AB   Exactly. So, as I was saying, there's a first Marx, who's the most Hegelian one, with a grand vision of history. Then, in my opinion, there's a completely different Marx, who really attempts to construct a science of society along with a theory of society's real functioning. As he himself said, this theory doesn't derive from the philosophy of history but from English political economy. It doesn't come from Hegel but from Ricardo. As is well known, Marx devoted almost all his time to writing *Capital*, which he never finished, moreover, and which is based on extremely detailed, extremely analytical scientific research, in which the Hegelian dialectic ultimately plays only a minor role. I'm not saying it disappeared completely, but it doesn't play a major role. The leading role is played by the analysis of the mechanisms of surplus value and its redistribution.

PE   But without the immanent logic of the philosophy of history.

AB The immanent logic of the mechanisms of surplus value and its redistribution is a logic of function.

PE Isn't it a logic of crisis?

AB It's more of a functional logic, in the final analysis.

PE But one that leads to crisis in the third book of *Capital*.

AB But the theory of cyclical crises isn't something Marx invented either. The idea that the mechanisms of capitalist society produce cyclical crises of overproduction can already be found in Adam Smith. This is a Marx who was intent on discovering the laws of capital's functioning and providing an analytical overview of them. I don't think this Marx was dialectical at all; he was analytical. There's not a shadow of a doubt that this is a Marx who was absolutely driven by the ideal of science, of positivist science.

PE What did this analytical Marx add to Smith?

AB What he added were conclusions he drew from the fact that the absolute crux of the matter was surplus value, the analytical and normative conclusions he drew from the fact that, when all is said and done, the basic law is to maintain at all costs the rate of profit. This would explain the various vicissitudes of social and political organization. So he introduced some significant new ideas, even as compared with Ricardo, but they were in the same spirit. And this Marx was a great nineteenth-century scientist.

And then there's a third Marx, who was a man of politics. This is the Marx who was the founder of the International, speaking out on specific episodes of class struggle in France, waging extremely complicated battles against the anarchists, against Proudhon, and so on. And this Marx used the two other Marxes when necessary, and he used the philosophy of history when he needed to. Naturally, he also used the debate over the science of economics, but the aim he pursued was an aim of a third type. The first type was the great aim to provide a sort of general framework for the evolution of history; the second was to provide an extremely precise analytics of the mechanisms of contemporary society; and the third was to create a tool for revolution, something that could actively contribute to the overthrow of the established order. This, after all, is the Marx who started out as a revolutionary in Germany. This Marx initiated something else yet again. I think that there is always a question in the Marxist tradition as to which Marx the various different Marxists are mainly referring to. It depends on the time, the period, the people, and even the texts that are being used. The texts that were kept hidden, that were banned, play a big part. In the French Communist Party milieu, for thirty years, people weren't allowed to read the *Manuscripts of 1844*. They were banned. They were regarded as Hegelian texts. Indeed, as you can see when you read them, the *Manuscripts of 1844* are texts that attempt to combine Marx 1 and 2 and ultimately to deposit that combination into Marx 3, that is, to make the proletariat the historical subject that enables the philosophy of history and the analytical vision of capitalism to be melded together.

All of this is to say that Marx is a very fascinating, very interesting reference for me on account of this very complexity, since, at bottom, Marx is someone who attempted to produce a theory of the revolutionary subject in a context dominated by a structural dialectic, that is, in a context that did not automatically lend itself to the issue of the creation of a new political subject. So there was something like a conflict within Marx himself, a conflict that had to do with using either analytical or dialectical materials, depending on whether he was dealing with economics or with history, for purposes that, all things considered, he cared deeply about and whose aim was the construction and organized emergence of a new political subject.

When Althusser said there was ultimately no theory of the subject in Marx, it's because it can't be found in *Capital*. If you read *Capital*, you're not going to find the new political subject: as we know, Marx stopped writing *Capital* when he got to the concept of classes. He was still far from dealing with the political subject. So the political subject can't be garnered from *Capital*. It can, however, be used in the context of the construction of the subject. I think Marx already represented a first attempt to ask how a structural analytics could be combined with the dialectic in such a way that it makes possible or sheds light on the question of the subject. That's why I'm so attuned to it, since I'd say that this is the problem that concerns me, too: how can I practice the most rigorous formal mathematics in such a way that it can ultimately be used for the question of the subject? That was already what Marx was attempting to do, and in some respects it was what Freud was attempting to do, too, as Lacan has clearly shown. In Freud there is also a theory, a very strong analytical bent, and thermodynamic models to explain the unconscious. He was a diehard positivist, as was Marx, in fact, and as were all the nineteenth-century thinkers, but, in the end, what nevertheless emerged from this was a new vision of the human subject. It was an unprecedented vision of the human subject, as Lacan later showed. When you come right down to it, they were dealing with the problem of having to push the structural analysis to the point where its truth itself required there to be something like a subject. And I think that what can be found in Marx and Freud, what they have in common, paradoxically, is that they are both subjectivizing positivists.

PE But how can a subject be imagined in a structural analysis?

AB   There will necessarily have to be a category of rupture.

PE   Yes, that's necessary.

AB   Absolutely. In Marx, it will be the category of "revolution," because revolution is an event that's neither necessary nor impossible; it's a possibility. But, contrary to what he has been made to say, Marx never thought this possibility was inevitable, absolutely necessary, and that it was going to occur all by itself. He wouldn't have spent all his time building an International under extremely difficult circumstances if he had thought as much. And with Freud there's this extraordinary idea of the analytic treatment that, at some point, will result in the subject's really changing his/her system of symptoms and psychical organization. In my more philosophical system it's the category of the event that encompasses all this, namely, this outside impetus, which, at some point, disrupts what the analytic has revealed. It's just that, to really understand the rupture, you also need to hold on to the analytic, because the rupture is the rupture of that structure, of that analytic, and it will preserve some particular features of it. In other words, the intelligibility of the rupture's consequences still requires you to bear in mind and have an understanding of the structure that was affected by the rupture. I think these are precisely the problems of revolutionary Marxism: how, under conditions of revolution, rupture, and so on, can the analytical and dialectical rigor of the previous analyses still be preserved? Because even though there's of course a rupture, the problem, which Marx moreover clearly envisaged when he analyzed the situations in France, is that no rupture is *total*. The rupture always occurs at one particular point, which may possibly spread out, but it always occurs at one particular point. So, in reality, there's the rupture, but everything surrounding the rupture, this point of rupture, is captured and embedded in what the structural analysis has revealed.

PE One can wonder, then, if there's a logic leading to the description of the revolutionary subject, whose definition would derive from these two activities, the analytical one and the dialectical one, and all of whose components Marx brought to bear in his political work.

AB I think the subject's nature is actually only experienced or partly revealed retrospectively. The subject is the very movement whereby the consequences of the evental rupture are drawn, in an intellectual, mental, etc., context, which is found in the situation. As regards the communist movement, it is clear that the subject elucidates the consequences of a revolutionary rupture by using dialectical philosophy, the analytic of Capital, a vision of the history of humanity, the examples provided by earlier revolutions and insurrections, and so on. The subject makes its way by using all the tools available to render the process underway intelligible. This intelligibility is always partial, because it's the movement that's primary. The consequences of the rupture operate freely: they are creative, they are active, and there's always a complicated relationship, which used to be the well-known problem of the relationship between theory and practice in the good old Marxist days, which weren't really as good as all that! As you yourself well know!

PE That's something else, it's a different issue!

AB I'm well aware of that, but, still, you do remember theory and practice, don't you?

PE Yes, I remember.

AB Everyone knew that it was the major problem nonetheless, that there was theory and practice. It was a bit abstract, of course, but that's what you used to learn in worn-out old Marxism-Leninism. Still, it's the real problem, just as in psychoanalysis there's a recurrent problem of the relationship between the progress of the treatment, the interpretations, the general theory of the unconscious, and so on. I think it's only natural that there should be such a problem, if it's assumed that a real movement of truth and subject – the two are interrelated – occurs from within through a rupture affecting a structure we've gained an understanding of through analytical and/or dialectical means. This understanding will be all the greater the less the analytical and dialectical dimensions are separated. I think this is a real problem, which we've inherited.

PE That means both are necessary, theory *and* practice.

AB Yes, both are necessary, and I think the concept of formalization – formalizing the experience, giving it its form – is probably the most important operator, because formalization is something that doesn't decide between analytical and dialectical. A dialectical-type formalization is conceivable and so is a more analytical one. Formalization doesn't decide; it leaves open the question of which one is dominant, and it avoids the conflict that has always existed between them. This is one of the truly important objectives of my philosophy. What I attempt to do is to show that, for specific issues, the apparent contradiction between analytical and dialectical thinking can be resolved, provided you're dealing with a real movement. In the context of a real movement, you can use either analytical elements or dialectical elements. The main issue is how to formalize this real movement, what form to give it. The notion of form is neither dialectical nor analytical in itself. It can sustain both, on a case by case basis. It's complicated, but I think that, in my philosophy, I attempt to provide additional resources for real movements, movements of access to the infinite, different opportunities to gain access to the infinite, so as not to be caught up in the conflict between the analytical and the dialectical. That was the conflict, in Marxism, between those who thought that there was a primacy of economics – and that everything ultimately depended on the economic analysis – and those who thought there was a primacy of political action and revolutionary activity. This conflict between ultra-left activism and rightwing economism was truly the bane of historical Marxism. It was also the bane of psychoanalysis, pitting those who thought it was basically an objective form of medicine against those, on the contrary, who aligned it completely with the pure theory of the subject. I want to get beyond that. Perhaps the clearest definition of my philosophical objectives is to show that the subject emerges in a real movement and that this real movement is dictated by a rupture within certain types of structures, certain types of analytical determinations. And to explain this process, to formalize it, the resources of dialectical analysis – in terms of negativity, critique, and contradiction – and analytical elements – in terms of structure, dominant elements of the structure, and so on – can both be used, by employing categories that are more in line with the different sorts of formalization.

PE So was Marx a man of politics, a revolutionary? Is there a political necessity that emerges from his dialectical work and from his analytical work?

AB Sure. As is clear when you read him, he gives us examples.

PE Examples that are evidence of a revolutionary Marx?

AB I think so.

PE Is that the crucible of your "communist Idea"?

AB Yes, but as a matter of fact, the communist Idea is neither an analytical nor a dialectical idea, strictly speaking. There's a dialectical version of it, if you consider the Marx of the *Communist Manifesto*, for example.

PE Is there a disconnect between dialectical and analytical work and the "communist Idea"? What's the relationship between them?

AB In my view, the communist Idea is the very example of an idea whose use is that of formalizing the real movement. It's an idea that allows you to judge the political value of a concrete situation or a real movement and whether its general orientation is homogeneous with the idea or not. From that point of view, it's a norm, and it's neither dialectical nor analytical. It's dialectical if you align communism with the philosophy of history, if you say that communism is the inevitable goal, the inevitable purpose of the movement of history from primitive societies to the present day, if it's understood as a category of the philosophy of history. But if you say that communism is the necessary, positive outcome that has gradually been created by capitalism itself and that there will be either communism or barbarism – either a catastrophe for the life of humanity or communism – you're connecting communism to the analytical element, i.e., you're linking it to the crises of capitalism. From that point of view, communism is something that serves to formalize the real movement, to indicate that the real movement is geared more towards the communist Idea. You're not forced to choose between analytical and dialectical: that's the advantage. I think it's a formal idea in a twofold sense: owing to the fact that it makes it possible to identify the general form of the current political movement, and in the sense that it's also normative. This means it allows you to judge or valorize certain situations over others, or certain tendencies within the situations over other tendencies. Marx moreover used the idea of communism this way in his most synthetic texts, those in which formalization is at work, in which he analyzed concrete political situations, such as the Paris Commune, class struggle in France, or the final episodes of the political struggle in Russia. The fact is, when you read these texts, it's clear that it's not a matter of chapters of the philosophy of history or of economic analyses but of establishing a formalization of a real movement, which renders what happened intelligible and, ultimately, shows the power of analysis and judgment that the communist Idea can bring to bear.

PE Is it a retrospective formalization? Is the "communist Idea" the formalization of the social movement?

AB No, whenever you act, whenever there's a real movement, you're always formalizing it, you're forming an idea of it. It's not something that happens afterwards. The people of Marx's International took part in the Paris Commune. The text about the Paris Commune was written by Marx – we have his notes – and it was written *during* the Commune, not afterwards. And so, day after day, Marx attempted to give it form, to find out what was happening and what the relationship was between what was happening there in Paris and the communist Idea. In that sense, he was a witness to the events. He was a participant in them, too, and just because he wasn't actually in Paris doesn't mean that he wasn't a mental participant. He was precisely an individual involved in the events.

PE So the communist Idea derives from action and reflection on the action?

AB But, in politics, action and reflection on the action are necessarily synchronous since you have to decide what you're going to do tomorrow. You have to have a form, you have to give form to what happened today.

PE   So the communist Idea isn't a normative idea that's applied from outside?

AB   No, not at all. It's an idea that's internal to the issue and can be shifted dialectically, if you will, onto a historical horizon or, on the contrary, be focused analytically on a very immediate, concrete situation. It has this twofold capacity, and, because of this, it's useful and is really a political idea. It's not just either an ideological idea or a statist idea. This is very clear in Marx's texts.

PE   It's not a philosophical idea?

AB   It's philosophical if you ask what philosophy can say about modern forms of politics. The category of "communism" would be developed philosophically, as it already was, moreover, in Marx, to designate what is capable of being subjectivated, of having a universal value, in contemporary forms of politics. Philosophy, in my view, is in reality only concerned with the absolute. What I've never been able to understand is what the philosophies that deconstruct the category of the absolute were all about, because I've always thought that it was bogus, that they secretly retained the figure of the absolute within its deconstruction. Thus, what will be of interest to philosophy when it provides political examples – "communism" will be one of their possible names but not the only one – is precisely everything in politics that has to do with the emancipation of humanity as a whole and hence the possibility that something about collective life has a universal value. Obviously, capitalism can't qualify.

PE Does the Idea of communism define communism? If the Idea of communism is something that comes into being and follows the political process, it's a political idea, linked to the political process. Does the Idea also have normative components or parts, and is that also true of the process?

AB It's important to understand that, as a formalization procedure, it only operates in the context of the implementation of analytical and dialectical categories. If it's isolated or separated from the analytical and dialectical materials provided by real situations, it ends up becoming merely a sort of vague historical horizon. When that happens, it's swallowed up by a philosophy of history. Often, the word "communism" need not even be involved. In Marx's analyses, the word "communism" doesn't play a crucial operational role; it's simply the point from which analytical operators can be made to operate on the state of production, classes, and so on, and can be simultaneously combined with dialectical operators that show how negativity works in all this, how contradictions war with each other. Moreover, the advantage and force of the word "communism" lie in the fact that it explicitly and deliberately denotes the conviction that a radically different organization of society is possible. This is a key point: it's for this reason that the word "communism" has become important again, because it denotes, among other things, the conviction that a type of societal organization different from the one that's dominant today is possible.

PE Wouldn't it be preferable to choose some other concept, given History's implication in all this?

AB But there isn't any other. Historically, there isn't any other that I know of, and the fact that communism was synonymous with aberrations for a while is not, in my opinion, a fundamental argument. People ask how I can maintain such a thing, but the Socialist states lasted fifty or seventy years, and that's an extremely short period of time.

PE That's one way of looking at it.

AB Obviously, for you in the GDR, it was a long time.

PE Granted, there's no other concept, but are there other forms of politics perhaps?

AB That's really like saying that the Inquisition was the essence of Christianity. You wouldn't accept such a thing. So don't accept it for communism either. Stalin's not the essence of communism. It's not because Stalin aligned himself with communism that he's the essence of communism. Stalin represents one particular historical period.

PE I think that considering the Inquisition to be the essence of Christianity and Stalinism to be

47

the essence of communism isn't just a question of conviction. It requires an argument.

AB But I'm all ready to discuss the arguments, which have to do with a specific and, moreover, very important issue: the issue of the state. That's the key point. Initially, we're not dealing with a simple relationship between ideology, politics, movement, truth, and so on. We're dealing with a unique and special question of the political field and the issue of the state. Incidentally, this is true for the Inquisition as well. The problem of Christianity was Constantine. Constantine was already a sort of Stalin, you might say. He was an example of those times when a political truth procedure merges with power under terroristic conditions. Actually, it would seem that any emancipatory doctrine is exposed, at one point or another, to this kind of danger. This experience is always negative: because of its pure and simple fusion with state power, the revolutionary political leadership is profoundly corrupted. This is understandable in a certain way because there's an absolutely fundamental assumption, we shouldn't forget, within the communist Idea: the withering away of the state. Marx and the communists knew perfectly well that there was a strategic incompatibility between the communist Idea and state power, since the communist Idea was only historically viable in their eyes provided state power was eliminated. And so it's hardly surprising that, in the long run, the exercise of state power ended up in practically intolerable contradictions with the communists.

PE But is it possible to imagine a society without a state?

AB There's no need to imagine anything; the point is to fight.

PE But when the state is protecting non-communist society, is it possible to fight without using terrorism?

AB For the time being, we're a long way from having to deal with that problem. We can't require that action should only be taken when we have a complete picture of the future – that's impossible. What we know is very clear. We know the conditions under which the Idea merged with a state power in the twentieth century – under

49

a name that was moreover not "communism," may I remind you; the term that was used was "socialist" states. This figure reminds us that communism is first and foremost a *movement*. It was perhaps Mao who put it most clearly: "Without a communist movement there is no communism." So communism can't be a power, strictly speaking; it has to be a movement. And that can't be something separate, the way the state is, or the way the party, or the party-state, ultimately is. Therefore, we need to be concerned at all times with the way communism exists as a movement. That's the lesson we can learn from this for the time being. It is within the figure of what the communist movement is that we can approach the question of the state and power again in a completely different way. For the time being, there's nothing anymore. So that takes us back to Marx. What I often say is that we're very close to the Marx of 1840–1850. A whole historical stage of the movement launched by Marx has come to an end. Capitalism has regained the upper hand all over the world; it is absolutely unrestrained and barbaric vis-à-vis the community. Since that barbarism is dominant for the time being, what we first need to do is rehabilitate the Idea and promote the word "communism" again. We need to organize small groups of local political experimentation. We need to be involved in the mass movements in Egypt and China, and so on. We need to support all of this with dialectical, analytical, and formal work. That's what the situation is.

PE   So you're not embarrassed by the history of the socialist states?

AB   Not in the least. I'm the first to be extremely interested in the history of the socialist states. But that phase is over. So we can't keep being told over and over that, since that phase was what it was, we should just keep quiet. That's after all what they tell us. Basically, everyone knows what the socialist states were like and that that situation won't happen again, that it's over. There's not a single person who says they're communist anymore, except possibly me and some friends of mine.

PE   No, in Germany *Die Linke* does. Do you know who they are?

AB   Sure I know who they are. I've even read the text written by the young members of *Die Linke* in which they said that the GDR had been very good. But that's not going to help them establish a new GDR. Besides, just between us, it took the Soviet army, first and foremost, to establish the GDR.

PE   True enough.

AB   A foreign army shouldn't be used to establish anything, and a foreign army should especially not be used to establish democracy anywhere.

PE   Speaking of democracy, in a conversation with Slavoj Žižek that was published under the title *Philosophy in the Present* (Polity, 2009) you said that everyone criticizes capitalism, that it's easy to do but it's not enough, and it's much more important to be concerned with the notion of democracy. In that context, what did you mean by that? Could you be more specific?

AB   I think that what we call democracy is simply the organization of the power of the dominant hegemony. It's the process that legitimizes or establishes domination. We have to stop concerning ourselves with it; it's the politics of the established order. The politics existing under the name of democracy isn't democratic at all. Do people have any power? No, as everyone is well aware, they have no power today, absolutely none. The people who do have power are, as we all know, the bankers and the politicians who are in cahoots with them. So we need to organize totally different kinds of political experiments and, to that end, it's not enough just to complain that capitalism is evil. That's not going to create new political organizations and experiments. Everyone complains that capitalism is evil, but then, as soon as elections are held, they go and vote for the established order.

PE   Can you imagine other kinds of political forms, forms of democracy, under capitalism?

AB   Democracies are dominant in the capitalist countries.

PE   In Germany, for example, there are institutions aimed at protecting human rights.

AB Yes, OK. There are advanced political forms where capitalism is advanced, because, as I pointed out, democratic parliamentary forms have been established in the old capitalist powers in Europe and America. In the "emerging powers," as they're called today, things are a bit more authoritarian. There's nothing surprising about that: things were more authoritarian in France, too, under Napoleon III. In the stages of primitive accumulation of capital the regime tends to be totalitarian.

PE You don't think there's been any progress, shall we say, for the people living in these "emerging" countries?

AB Progress, now, as far as I'm concerned, is in the future. I see no reason to fight for China to be democratic; I couldn't care less. It will become democratic all by itself when it's rich enough, that's all. And that's the history of capitalism itself; it's not *my* history of it. Once China has an imperialist productive capacity along with a strong army and has perhaps won a war against the United States, the way we fought a war against Germany, it will treat itself to a parliament. That's what human history today is like. When you have a heavily armed, imperialistic, dominant power that's not afraid of war, you can establish that type of political regime. In reality, what we call democracy is the system of government that's suited to the most developed forms of contemporary capitalism.

PE   But it still makes a difference to people whether they live in China or not, doesn't it?

AB   Of course it makes a difference.

PE   Isn't there a case for improving people's situation there?

AB   Just because it makes a difference doesn't mean that capitalism in the West is a norm. Imperialist capitalism is still a form of capitalism. In recent times, the Americans have killed more people than the Chinese have, in Iraq, for example. So this shouldn't be seen through rose-colored glasses. The imperialist powers are the ones that have powerful armies. They openly loot Africa – they're predators – and they use that to buy off a portion of public opinion in their countries. So there's nothing surprising about it. There's nothing really of interest to me about it. None of that points society in an egalitarian direction, a communitarian direction. There's nothing that's related to the communist Idea. What's more, I think it's a pathology.

PE A pathology?

AB I think capitalism is pathological. It's utterly outrageous that such enormous amounts of wealth are grabbed up by a very small continent. It's a pathology, a disease. Ultimately, everyone thinks that China is getting sicker and sicker and that it will become a great power under the conditions of what we already know to be the essence of the great powers. So China's development is of no intellectual interest to me; it's all mapped out. China will become an imperialistic, nuclear power, dominating the world market and looting Africa; it has already begun to do so. And later it will become a place of big alliances with an affluent middle class. It will bring in immigrants – Africans, for example. I'm not interested in a world that is solely focused on wanting that country to be like us. That's completely wrong.

There's no reason to want everyone else to become like us.

PE I can understand that argument, but there's a difference between us that comes from the difference between our lives. I, for example, have lived in a country where I've experienced what it's like to have no legal means to protect myself as a free citizen. Because of that, I can appreciate when there's a difference and some progress. Everything I do now, I'm able to do thanks to the fact that I broke out of prison and escaped from that non-capitalist political system.

AB That difference does exist. I agree that living in France is completely different from living in Cameroon.

PE Or in East Germany back then.

AB Besides, many Cameroonians feel the same way, and they've come here to live, just to be able to live. But even if capitalism is a historical stage of production, in terms of the basic norms of thought it's a pathology, even if a pleasant one, pleasant for those who live within it. You can't accept it as a political norm if you're for a minimum degree of "health." As for the type of life this society offers, you don't have to look very hard to see that it's an extremely destructive society. It's perfectly clear that it's not conducive to anything that has a universal value, that it's hostile to equality, that, little by little, it's destroying the figure of education, and that it's actually hostile to truths, that it's a regime of opinions.

2

24 March 2012

PE Yesterday we discussed the subject. We situated it in the history of philosophy and put it back in the context of the 1950s to 1960s. What I'm interested in now, after our critical comments about it, are the consequences, the possibilities opened up by this concept of subject as you develop it. I think it's a concept you feel very strongly about.

AB I think I said that the subject is what makes it possible for the individual to have access to the infiniteness of the real, to the infinity of the real. I also said that the subject is what enables the individual, who is singular, particular, to have access to the universal. The concept of the subject is linked to this capacity, this possibility for the individual no longer to be solely at the service of his/her particularity – what we call his/her interests, in today's world – but also to be involved in, to take an active role in, the construction of something that has a universal value or something that touches the infinity of the real. Thus, the subject is a concept denoting a sort of mediation, or intermediary, or, more precisely, intermediate movement, between the particular, individual, biological, cultural, and national limitations of the individual and something that has a universal value, which is close to infinity and, from that point of view, is beyond this original limitation. What's important to understand is that the process whereby the individual is incorporated into a subject, or which enables the individual to be a subject, nevertheless always occurs in a particular world. So the subject is a sort of movement that, within the particular, gains access to the universal. And it does so with particular materials.

Let me give a very simple example. Suppose we talk about poetic creativity – let's not always talk about politics, which is often boring! So let me back up a bit. We said that the subject is the moment when the individual embraces a possibility that transcends his/her singularity, his/her particularity, and creates or builds something whose value may be universal or whose real may be infinite. But what I wanted to point out is that, even so, this is not a transition to a different world, as in Plato.

PE Yes, that's important.

AB It's very important. The individual remains particular, and truth itself is produced in a particular world, with particular materials. I was using the example of poetry, of the poetic creative process. A poem is written by a great poet, read to other people, heard, admired, and so forth. However, at the beginning it wasn't written in a universal language; it was written in German or French or English. Likewise, if a painter depicts the outside world, it's the outside world of a specific historical period. The people wear particular types of clothing, and a great religious painting, for example, refers to the Christian context.

What I mean by this is, just because a work of art may ultimately have universal value doesn't mean that it has left behind the world in which it was created. It, its material, and its situation remain particular, and that's why we speak of the art of the Western Middle Ages, or of Arab art, or of German poets, and so on. The problem is how a work, a work of art – let's take that example – can have universal significance, i.e., from a certain perspective, be addressed to all of humanity even though its production, its situation, and its subject matter are particular. To explain this, we can't resort to the idea that there are two worlds, a material one and a transcendent or spiritual one, since the fact of the matter is that ordinary individuals can have access to this world and this subject.

PE They have access because they have the capacity for universality.

AB Yes, but I think that it's slightly more complicated than that. How is it that a great poem, written in German, for example, can be perceived by a French person as a poem with universal power even though it has been translated, transformed, and so on? I don't know German and yet I know that Hölderlin is a great poet, and I know this because I've read Hölderlin's poems in French. Hence, I haven't really read

Hölderlin's poem as such, I've read something that comes from Hölderlin's poem but has been transformed. And so there is indeed something in that poem that's not reducible to the German language in which it was written. It was written in the German language and it wouldn't exist without the German language.

PE It's not reducible to the material conditions of its emergence.

AB To explain this point, we obviously have to go back to the notion of rupture that we talked about last time. In fact, a great work of art, an invention, a creation, is something that, within particular conditions, necessarily transcends those particular conditions. This is what I've called an immanent exception. It's an exception that's internal; it's not an external exception. And so if particular works are capable of having a universal value it's because they are not entirely reducible to the particular conditions of their creation but are also an immanent exception *within* these conditions. They therefore reveal not just the concrete conditions of their existence but also a rupture within these conditions.

So they're actually also events; they're not just internal particularities. Something in them is at variance with the material conditions of their emergence. If it were otherwise we wouldn't understand – this is a question Marx poses in the preface to the *Grundrisse*, I believe – why we are moved by Greek tragedies, or why we find Greek mythology so fascinating, when it was a society completely different from our own. And, as is well known, Marx says: What are Zeus' lightning bolts, after all, compared with our cannons, with our steam engines, with electricity? And, in my opinion, he gives a wrong answer to what, for him, is a genuine question, because if human consciousness is the product of social conditions, then it's hard to understand why Greek tragedy is so powerful. That's a question, a genuine question. And he answers it by saying that it's because we're always attuned to our childhood, and the Greek world is the childhood of humanity. That's a weak answer, as we clearly sense. Marx himself probably knew it was weak; that's why he asked the question. I think we need to see that there is indeed something universal in the Greek tragedies, which means something other than the fact of our being in the historical context of their production. We're not citizens of Athens; we certainly don't think the same way as a citizen of Athens did. It's just that we're moved by *Antigone* or by *Oedipus Rex* because there's something in *Antigone* and *Oedipus Rex* that's an immanent exception to Greek culture in its strict particularity. So we'll call "creation," generally speaking, this immanent exception, this possibility of the immanent exception, which moreover accounts for the fact that a lot of Greek things won't really move us while others will move us because they were already, in their own time, out of sync, like an event within the world as it was.

So, to return to your question, the subject's potential is this, the immanent exception, the possibility for an individual to participate in an immanent exception and consequently no longer to be a pure and simple product of his/her own concrete conditions, his/her own family, background, education. S/he is all of those things. In a sense, s/he is really all of those things, but s/he also has the possibility, from within them all, to become involved in a process that's a little different. A very simple example I already gave, which takes us back to politics, is, as everyone could see at the time of the Arab uprisings, that there were people involved who had no idea that they were capable of anything of the sort. A Cairo shopkeeper, minding his own business, suddenly became an actor in history.

PE For anyone who knew Cairo, it was hard to imagine such a thing.

AB Exactly, it was unexpected. However much the situation in Egypt is analyzed, the fact is, something like that can't be predicted. It happened in actual fact, but it's not true that it had to happen, and yet everyone knows that it really did happen. So there's also the idea of a beginning in the immanent exception, and it's not just Egyptian society or, in my artistic example, Greek society; it's also, within that Egyptian or Greek society, something that is beginning. That beginning may not last, but it's not just a result of the past; it's also a pure present, a radical beginning, a beginning that can't be inferred from the past.

PE Is there an analogy between a beginning like that in society and the beginning that occurs in the creative subject?

AB It's the same thing: there's that evental beginning. And what will happen to the subject is that it will be caught up in the event, the beginning. It will be taken over by the beginning. Instead of remaining what it is in its social conditions, it will take part in, be summoned by, the event, as if something were beginning. Moreover, when you ask someone who's taking part in a demonstration of this sort, s/he'll immediately tell you that something is beginning for him/her, too. People always say: "I would never have believed I could do such a thing." It's a new world that's beginning. Ultimately, every great universal work is in its own way a beginning. That's why we can begin with it. We don't have to know everything about Greek society or live in Greek society or believe in the Greek gods to be moved by *Oedipus Rex* or *Antigone*. We're moved because, in those works, we discover a trace of the beginning of a new idea, a new vision, or a new form, in the case of art. Thus, the subject is always the agent of something of that sort, that is, of something that, for the individual, is like the beginning of an exception to his/her ordinary way of being.

PE   That's really nice, really positive. It gives us hope.

AB   But I'd like to stress the fact that it exists, that it's a real experience. I experienced it politically in the month of May 1968 and everything that followed. Actually, you experience it every time you discover a work of art that moves you, that overwhelms you. When you read a novel, you're captivated, you're seized, you're inside that world.

PE   We've all had that experience.

AB   Everyone can have the experience. It's the same as when you fall in love. These are moments when, maybe not for very long – but that's just it: you're experiencing a living exception to the ordinary order of things – you become someone who's not reducible to the concrete conditions of his/her existence, because you've touched the real of the exception. And in the process you've also begun something. We can speak of the becoming-subject – the subject of the work of art, the subject of a political uprising. The experience I often refer to is when you suddenly

68

understand a mathematical proof. It's something that frightens people, because mathematics is very scary. I do mathematics, I know it very well, and I know that it's very complicated. You've struggled, you haven't really understood, and then all of a sudden you get it, and it's really as though the sun had come up. This is really a perfect experience of the moment when, all at once, you find yourself in the universal. Before, you were feeling your own, unique limitations, then, by dint of working, of keeping at it, of plugging away, you can experience that subjective metamorphosis whereby you're in an element in which everything becomes clear, everything becomes transparent. At the same time, what has happened is truly universal, because the mathematician who discovered the proof introduced it him/herself into that universality. That's what a subject is.

PE I understand very well. I'd say the same thing about philosophy. I remember when I was young, I was very fascinated by Hegel. At first I couldn't understand a thing about his whole construction, especially the beginning . . .

AB   . . . which is at the end!

PE   For a long time I couldn't understand, but after a few years of reading Hegel, it all became clear, and I could read Hegel as easily as a newspaper. Something had happened. It wasn't an act; it was an event. Frankly, I was surprised by my sudden ability to understand.

AB   That's right, and I think we have to say that that possibility – since you were talking about potentiality – is what it means to be progressive. To be progressive is to claim that any individual has the ability to participate in something like that, in different ways. The amorous, or scientific, or artistic, or political ways are different from one other; they have different conditions.

PE   When you say "participate" are you referring only to production, or do you put production and reception on the same plane?

AB   Actually, to really participate in the reception of something is to re-experience the beginning of its production. That's exactly what we were saying. When you understand the mathematical proof, it's because you've done it yourself. When you really understand *The Phenomenology of Spirit* it's as if you had written it yourself.

PE I see. That's really nice.

AB When you see a painting and all of a sudden it fascinates you and you go on standing in front of it because something becomes clear from it, it's the same thing. The painter is speaking to us, s/he's right beside us, and we are beginning something with him/her. Now, of course, creation sometimes has something more intense, more particular, about it, but I think reception and creation absolutely have to be brought into line with each other. It's important to understand that the experience of reception of the universal is also an experience in which the subject enters the universal. The example I gave of the mathematical proof is typical of this, but there are also those of *The Phenomenology of Spirit*, the painting, the poem, or anything at all. And that's why this possibility is open to everyone, exactly, in fact, like the way students, shopkeepers, workers, and so on all found themselves on Tahrir Square in Cairo and had the profound feeling of their equality at that moment. Equality before what? Before the fact that they were undergoing a new birth. They were all in the process of being born together to something – they didn't know exactly what, but that's another problem, the problem of consequences. Once the subject has entered something of this sort, it will make something of it; there will be consequences. For example, even with you, after you had understood Hegel, there were consequences. There are consequences, including the fact that one begins to have doubts.

PE   I'm only talking about the moment that's a new beginning.

AB   Hegel will lead to something else afterwards. Hegel is there, he's in your mind, and you'll work with him, or maybe against him at some point, but working against him or with him comes to the same in the end.

PE   But what about participating in something universally negative? I'm thinking of the Nazi era, for example.

AB It should be noted that there was something objectively anti-universal in Nazi ideology: that was the whole point, after all. Nazism was the promotion of German particularity as such.

PE I see it the same way, but I was thinking about that emotion, that euphoria.

AB Yes, but careful: in my opinion, the euphoria, the feeling of communitarian participation, is absolutely insufficient when it comes to characterizing the subject because the representation of what the participants are involved in must really have a universal vocation in their eyes. The content of the representation is very important. The participation must have an explicitly universal vocation. If you understand the mathematical proof, you know that that proof is for everyone. You understood it precisely because it can be understood by everyone, whereas if you're gathering together to scream "Death to the Jews!" it's not the same. In that case, on the contrary, it's negativity that prevails. That's an aspect we haven't discussed. I think the subject is an *affirmative* power.

PE That dimension does have to be added, I think, because otherwise there might be confusion.

AB It has to be added precisely because we were talking about enthusiasm. But enthusiasm doesn't suffice to characterize the subject – that's a good example. The most important point is the penetration into the sort of universal light in which you know deep down that if someone else understands the proof, s/he will understand the same thing as you do. That's extremely important. Likewise, when someone reads Hölderlin s/he won't necessarily interpret him the way you do, but Hölderlin's greatness will ultimately function the same way for both of you. Similarly, this is why there's always a sort of shared idea that's present in political demonstrations. The political demonstration tears you away from your particular conditions. It projects you into a space of universal openness, and the values you'll defend are values you know will attract universal sympathy. That's what happened with the Arab uprising, which everyone regarded as positive, whereas Nazism, which glorified particularity, wasn't an immanent exception; it was, on the

74

contrary, a fierce will to identity. Therefore, let's not confuse the enthusiasm for particularity – you were in fact right to raise the objection – and the enthusiasm kindled by being in immanent exception to particularity.

PE Yes, that distinction has to be made.

AB It's essential! On the other hand, I think that, from that perspective, we can explain the fact that the communitarian gathering as such is a simulacrum of an event, a false event. It's the very essence of falsification. I developed this point at some length in my little *Ethics* book, in which I defined precisely what a false event is, namely, something that presents itself as an event, that offers enthusiasm, but does so through the glorification of particularity instead of through the exception to particularity. The various fascisms obviously did so explicitly inasmuch as they took the categories of particularity as the fundamental category.

PE It was the same during my youth in East Germany. Every May Day there was a repetition of that false enthusiasm.

AB   It shouldn't have been the same, because, normally, communism isn't the glorification of a particularity. Fascism is the explicit glorification of a particularity: communism is never, in principle, the glorification of a particularity. It's the end of particularities; it's internationalism, not particularism.

PE   I participated in it because I was taken in by the falsification.

AB   Yes, sure, but the falsification occurred on a different level.

PE   But it was still a falsification, because the people who made a show of that enthusiasm were actually the petty bourgeois, who were attempting to defend their own power, their own interests.

AB   Yes, of course. I'm not saying it wasn't a falsification. It was on a different level, though, because the level of the explicit discourse wasn't nationalistic; it was internationalist. It wasn't for one particular class; it was for the end of classes. The explicit discourse was universalist, which wasn't at all the case with Hitler's discourse.

PE   So is the discourse definitional?

AB   No, I'm not saying the discourse is definitional. I'm saying that you have to take into account the fact that it wasn't the same discourse. The resemblance between communism and fascism is a mistaken resemblance. They're not at all alike.

PE   But at the level of the discourse there are some resemblances.

AB   Not only at the level of the discourse. The level of the discourse is never entirely separable from what happens. There are always areas of contact between them. Personally, I think the whole thing was a total failure: I'm not suggesting that the Socialist states be rehabilitated. That's not at all my view of things, but still, you have to admit that the Socialist states, which advocated world communism, were very different from people advocating the German race's superiority over all others.

PE   There's no question of rehabilitating them. As we both know, after World War II, in Russia but also in the East European countries, people were routinely tortured and killed.

AB   In actual fact, it was done in the name of a universal.

PE   How could that have happened in the name of universality? Was it an aberration?

AB   It was a matter of a universality that had become a pure particularity. That was the problem.

PE   However, this universality didn't pass itself off as a particularity but rather as a universality.

AB   No, but it's important to see what happened. They began by saying that universality was represented by a class, the proletariat.

PE   Which already no longer exists.

AB   Exactly, because when Marx wrote that the proletariat represents universality, he did so for a very specific, ontological, reason, namely that the proletariat is something that has no particular attribute, something's that nothing. So it's the universality of the negative. But in the Stalinist tradition "proletariat" became a representative substance, not just negativity. The proletariat was indeed supposed to represent universality, and then the Party was supposed to represent the proletariat, hence the Party was already a representation of representation. And, ultimately, Stalin represented the Party. The starting point was universality, but, little by little, through a succession of representations, it was changed into its opposite. In the end, one individual wound up representing the movement of universality. This necessarily led to a monstrous pathology, because it was an absolute forcing of conditions.

Clearly, when one individual represents universality, there is no longer any immanent exception. And the fundamental issue that interfered with it was the category of representation. Philosophically speaking, this was the big turning point, which, in my opinion, began in the late nineteenth century with the establishment of the social-democratic parties in Europe. Marx never entertained any such idea. The Party wasn't one of his ideas but an idea that came later, and it placed the notion of representation at the heart of political activity.

The notion of representation was in many respects at odds with the idea of the immanent exception, because the immanent exception creates a rupture in what there is. It doesn't claim that one element of what there is stands for all the others; that would be impossible. What was at issue was truly the idea of representation, which was moreover shared, in a sense, by the parliamentary democracies and the first socialist parties. The German Social-Democratic Party, which was the model, was at the same time a pillar of German parliamentarianism. The idea of representation, which completely perverted the idea of universal democracy, reached its peak in the Leninist, and later the Stalinist, construction of the party, where universality was really represented. It wasn't a question of universality in its movement as an immanent exception, in its subjective act. Rather, it was a question of a stable representation of universality in the form of the party, which was the representative of that universality.

PE   Did the break occur right away?

AB   In my opinion, it began around 1889–90, since there's a very specific passage in Marx's

Manifesto, which I always point out. Marx says that the communists are not a separate part of the general workers movement. They aren't; that's explicit. He gives two arguments for this. First, they're concerned with the movement as a whole and not just with one particular phase of the movement, which means they're already projected forward toward universality. And second, they're internationalists. Ultimately, what Marx called "the communists" is simply a conception within the general movement, and this conception was projected forward toward universality through the modality of, or the participation in, the overall movement and the International, two categories that were effectively universal. Starting in the years 1880–90, the German Social-Democratic Party became the general model, it has to be said. It was moreover the model for Lenin – and this was the beginning of something completely different – for whom the party was sanctified as the active representative of the proletariat. This sanctification of the party began very early on. Stalin didn't invent it; he was its heir. He was its ruthless heir, because the difference between Stalin and the others was that Stalin was in power; he held absolute power. Not only was political representation completely centralized, but, in addition, it was endowed with quasi-absolute power. So, in this case, the original universality of the Idea of communism became dialectically reversed into its opposite, and, I'm convinced, the operator of this reversal was the idea of representation.

PE It's really interesting to view the Social-Democratic Party as a break with universalism.

AB The emergence of German social-democracy is a historical phenomenon all by itself. Of course, some defects were already evident right from the time of Marx's International, but we needn't go back that far. Marx's International was by no means conceived of on the model of a social-democratic party. It was a fundamentally ideological attempt at organization by those within the different world workers movements who had attempted to have both of the features I mentioned above. Don't forget that, at the beginning, Stalin stood for communism in a single country, and, later, internationalism itself would end up as representation. What did the notion of the "fatherland of socialism" mean? Basically, just as the Party represented the proletariat and Stalin represented the Party, the Soviet Union represented internationalism as a nation. Moreover, it is very well known that, in reality, Soviet interests dictated everything else. And even with that, there's an idea of representation. The "fatherland of socialism" was the idea that socialism was represented somewhere, but this was totally contrary to the internationalist idea.

PE I understand your argument, but I have two questions, which can in fact be combined into one. Why did this shift – and this had already begun with Engels – occur in a politics established in organizations, and, as that politics was universalist in aim, why did it fall into the trap of representation? The other side of the question is, of course, whether the political expression of the universalist idea isn't necessarily representation and whether that can be avoided.

AB I think that, as usual, subjectivation is never entirely pure. We all know that no phenomenon is a pure phenomenon, precisely because we're not Platonists in the bad sense of the term. There is no pure Idea and impure world. No, there are always forms of representation that filter into politics.

Even if universality is an immanent exception, it is always at work within particularity; it operates within particularity. Even when I'm reading a poem by Hölderlin and I'm participating in a certain artistic universality, it's nevertheless *I* who am participating in it, and my past, my childhood, my desires, and so on will also come into play. So politics is at work within existing groups, and it would be more appropriate to speak about an ongoing struggle against representation than about the complete elimination of representation. The complete elimination of representation would be the elimination of the state, in fact, or the withering away of the state. That's a strategic line, but the struggle against representation is not compatible with the assertion that representation is the crux of the problem. You can't fight against representation and then say that the Party represents the proletariat, Stalin represents the Party, and so on. Thus, the struggle against representation is incompatible with a perfectly clear doctrine of representation, which was put in place in the late nineteenth century. The idea of a party of the proletariat was not Marx's idea, absolutely not. But from the late nineteenth century on, it became a dominant idea, an established idea, which, in my opinion, was related to the entry of the process of universality into the state, since the social-democratic parties were parties that began by engaging in elections, having a faction in the national assembly, and so on. All this was therefore linked to the emergence of modern parliamentarianism and to a general doctrine of representation. But I think the key moment was the defeat of the Paris Commune, which led to a negative assessment of all forms of revolutionary spontaneity. The slaughter was so horrendous, the defeat of the Commune was so bloody, that everyone thought they now needed to be better organized and more disciplined. Little by little, this became a dominant idea, and it's a basic fact of the history of politics that defeats are tragic, even more so in terms of their consequences than in terms of the actual event itself. The defeat of the Paris Commune gradually led most revolutionary militants to embrace the idea that a well-structured party was necessary, that representation was necessary.

PE Can the idea that, as a revolutionary militant you need a well-structured party, a representation, be reversed?

AB Sure it can be reversed. It's only now that we really know the overall assessment of what was learned from the defeat of the Paris Commune. That defeat was at the root of the principles developed by Lenin, including the idea that it was because of a strong, established, disciplined party that the revolution had been won. It's important to understand that, at a global level, the 1917 Revolution was experienced as revenge for the Paris Commune. The Paris Commune was crushed in blood, and in 1917 the Revolution was victorious. That's why it had such an amazing reverberation, which was felt even by you and me, you've got to admit. Why was that so? Everyone knew about Stalin, everyone knew about representation, but everyone was still affected by the echo of that absolutely unprecedented historical event, the victory of the Revolution. Nothing like it had happened since 1789. It was the second victorious revolution, and, like the first, it had an enormous, worldwide impact. But underlying it was the defeat of the Paris Commune.

Yet the Commune had many positive aspects that were completely overshadowed by its defeat. It was much less terroristic, much less geared toward the idea of representation, and much

86

more democratic in the basic sense of the word: it united factions that differed from one another but still worked together. Unfortunately, these ideas were crushed by the defeat. And this resulted in something that I place great emphasis on, something that could be called a military communism, because it was the military model that prevailed all throughout the twentieth century. It was the military model, or "barracks socialism," to use a phrase my friends and I employ.

The justification of this model, at the beginning, was the idea of being the winners in the insurrection, the victorious insurrection. This required an iron discipline, sacrifice, and so on – which isn't totally wrong – but later, it ended up being the model for society as a whole. Ultimately, Stalin stood for the attempt to build a military socialism on a nationwide scale, using violence, prison, torture, and the idea that if anyone was a problem, you killed them. It was that simple. It was a habit acquired in the civil war, too: if anyone was against you, you killed them. And this military socialism had representative roots, so to speak, soon after 1871. It impacted the whole latter part of the nineteenth century, and, truth be told, Lenin and Stalin were a bit like the

Russian version of this Western invention. Don't forget that, for Lenin, before he came into conflict with Trotsky, the great party, the model, was the German Social-Democratic Party.

PE   It's new for me to see that as the beginning.

AB   In any case, the problems emerged very early on. Look at texts like *Critique of the Gotha Program.* Marx and Engels aligned themselves with German social-democracy but at the same time felt that it wasn't right either.

PE   What lessons can be learned from this?

AB   I think that, for a long period of time, political experiments must accept to be decentralized, undisciplined, and non-violent, in a sense, or in any case as little violent as possible. But it's important to understand that the mindset at the time of the Third International was just the opposite. It was as violent as could be, even among the young people. It wasn't just the Soviet Union – even I once thought, at one point, that maybe violence was creativity, after all, that violence was the midwife of History, as Engels put it. I believe that today violence needs to be reined in, that we need to have the least violence possible or no violence at all, if possible. And as for discipline, yes, OK, but just subjective discipline, if you're taking part in a demonstration, not forced discipline, not barracks discipline, not hierarchical, military discipline with compulsory obedience. I often say that the big problem for politics today is inventing a non-military discipline, because discipline is necessary. The people have nothing but their discipline, after all. The others have money; they have weapons; they have the state apparatus. If you go on strike – to take a very simple example – if you go on strike in a factory, it works because there's discipline, because everyone agrees to go along with it. As is well known, if that's no longer the case, then the strike won't work. So discipline is necessary. But do you have to beat up people who refuse to strike? Do you have to "beat the crap" out of them? That was the mindset of the Third International. Let's "beat the crap" out of the guy who refuses to go on strike, that'll teach him.

PE   But that can be found today as well.

89

AB Sure. But I think it's a bad thing. I think that if the idea of going on strike is right, we should be able to talk it over with people. We should be able to talk it over with them one at a time, go over to their house and explain to them why it would be better to strike. Everything that was connected with obligation, constraint, and violence needs to be replaced patiently, point by point, with something else, which is ultimately the Socratic dialogue, after all (*laughing*). If it's right and if it's true, we should be able to convince the other person. We've got to start from this major philosophical idea.

PE But what if the other side responds with riot police? That's the reality, if you think about South America and the violence perpetrated against the farmers.

AB A rule can be made that a certain type of defensive violence is unavoidable. But it has to be defensive, meaning that you've got to be able to prove that you're defending something you've built, decided on, accomplished. Of course, I also think it's right for strikers to organize a picket line. The problem isn't that there's a picket line;

it's how the picket line behaves. That's an important distinction. And the idea of representation also needs to be kept in check at every level, including at the level of the leader.

PE That's the heart of the matter.

AB It's the key point. We're all well aware that leaders are needed, too, that in a complicated action there are people who organize to make decisions. But I'm absolutely opposed to secret leadership, to things the leaders keep to themselves. That was also an important aspect of the Third International: the leaders' decisions were taken in secret meetings. I think that, as a general rule, everything must or should be able to be revealed, except to the enemies. Things have to be out in the open, they have to be discussed, and there has to be discipline, but it shouldn't be based on the military model. To that end, local political experiments are necessary. For the time being, that's the situation. We can't organize some big global thing; that's just not the case. At the global level, what we can do is discuss the communist Idea. That's what I'm trying to organize: to discuss whether we can or should use that idea again or not, and what assessment, in this regard, should be made of Marx and the twentieth century. If this is useful and serves some purpose, it can be discussed at a global level with anyone. By contrast, in terms of concrete political experiments, I think we have to give local experiments the time to develop, and we should try to learn what they're about. What I kind of had in mind was to try to create a global space, a space that would simply be a place for exchanging experiences, where everyone would describe their own way of activating the idea of emancipation, what specific activities they've carried out, and how they've managed to keep violence in check. It would be a place to report on experiences that have been very interesting in this regard, including in very tense situations such as in Nepal and similar areas. There's a lot to report on and talk about if we're to enter a new era of politics that isn't a politics of representation.

PE You mean develop local politics as centers for experimentation?

AB Where what people describe has a universal value, where you can ask them questions.

PE That's currently happening in Germany, in Stuttgart, for example, with regard to the new train station, and there are several other small groups involved in this sort of politics.

AB Yes, we have some things in France, too, and there are really interesting things in the Asian countries. I'm optimistic: I think these things will continue and that we'll learn some new things. The lessons we're discussing here are already somewhat familiar: everyone knows we can't repeat what was done in the Soviet Union. But to come back to philosophy, we've got to oppose the notion of immanent exception to the notion of representation and show that they are really not at all the same sort of thing, even though, historically, the immanent exception has often been embedded in a representation. The classic example of this are the vicissitudes of the concept of proletariat, because "proletariat," in Marx's view, was an immanent exception. Although the proletariat worked in society, it wasn't acknowledged by society. It was overlooked or invisible in society; it had no responsibility. It was a subject that was claimed not to be a subject and was reduced solely to its labor power. The proletariat

was typically something that could not be represented. The idea of the party of the proletariat
is a complete paradox, and the history of that
paradox is a very long and terrible one. It is still
going on. So that's what I have to say about this
topic.

PE So we're back to politics again?

AB Yes, but I actually started with poetry.

PE Let's go back to poetry, to love, to the
family. Is the immanent exception found in other
fields? Can one be a subject in love, in creativity,
in mathematics?

AB I think it can easily be shown how a
new mathematical vision emerges by way of
an immanent exception to the existing state of
mathematics. There's a brilliant mathematician,
and a formidable thinker, too, the French mathematician Galois, who was the inventor of the
theory of groups. He basically said that every
great innovation in mathematics occurs on the
basis of what remained un-known in the prede-
cessors. The earlier mathematicians had thought,

as it were, something new, but weren't aware that they'd thought it. The new idea remained invisible in their work because they weren't able to draw any conclusions from it. They thought it without being truly aware they were doing so. All this provides us with a good description of the immanent exception. Mathematical discourse is totally explicit, and if there is something that remains un-known in it, it will be revealed in symptoms, incomplete proofs, or efforts that go nowhere. This explains why Galois' discovery of the concept of groups was linked to the state of mathematics in his time – particularity – and was at the same time at variance with, invisible in, or ultimately in exception to, what the mathematics of his times was propounding. Thus, "exception" is a very legitimate category. So is "representation," moreover, since, after a while, the new discovery becomes established, it becomes an educational subject – textbooks are written – and it consequently loses its creative capacity and becomes just a knowledge transmission tool.

PE The same thing happens in academic philosophy.

AB   Exactly, and these are also processes that I've tried to describe. I've shown how, in the sciences, there are people who cling to the status quo in science and don't see that it's changing. In the arts, it's academicism. In politics, representation is the State. In love, it's actually the defeat of love by family constraints. It's very clear that the threat hanging over the exception – the threat of the exception's return to the established order – can be described very precisely, at least in the four areas I call the four great truth procedures: the sciences, political innovations (the politics of emancipation), the arts, and love. Thereafter, we could say, more abstractly, that politics concerns the fate of the community, the "being together," as Hannah Arendt would say. The sciences concern knowledge, nature, and objective laws, and mathematics is the figure of thinking, of pure being. As for the arts, I think they concern the notion of form: what is a form? The arts always deal with the putting into form of the sensible material in various different spheres. They constitute the relationship between the sensible and form. The immanent exception in art is always the moment when something that was considered to be formless takes on form. Essentially, that's what happened at the time when non-figurative painting emerged. Before then, only a figure was considered a form. Un-figuration, the non-figurative, became a form in its turn, and that is a general model. The arts thus deal with this relationship to form. Last but not least, love, as I have argued, is the question of difference, the existential question of difference as immanent exception.

PE What distinguishes the family from love?

AB The family is to love what the state is to politics. It is both within and without. Besides, you can't be involved in politics without dealing with the state, as long as it exists, at any rate. But nor can you think that politics is state power, because that's Stalinism. It's the same with the family: you can't think of love without think-ing of the family, because, in the final analysis, the way love becomes established, its necessary regime of particularity, still involves cohabi-tation, children, the organization of time, and building a life together. But love can't be reduced to the family, either, because then you end up with a utilitarian vision.

PE Isn't the family the representation that threatens the immanent exception of love?

AB Absolutely. That's why I think that the family is the representation that threatens love *and* that this representation is partly unavoidable – exactly the way the state is the typical figure of representation in politics. Likewise, academicism is, in a sense, unavoidable in art, and yet it is its enemy.

PE That's just what I wanted to ask. So it's the same in all the different spheres?

AB In science, scientific academicism is the moment when science becomes a mere educational subject rather than a creative subject – even though education is obviously necessary.

PE Are there any strategies for protecting the immanent exception, even when we know that representation is unavoidable?

AB That's the big problem, the general problem, which I'd call the problem of organization. The immanent exception is actually always very

fragile. All you have to do is say the words "immanent exception" to understand how fragile the
concept is. As a rule, subjectivation tries not only
to embrace the immanent exception but also to
protect it, to draw and establish its consequences.
That's the reason why there's always something
organized – not representative but organized
– around the immanent exception. In art, the
example that could be given is the schools, such
as those of the surrealists or the symbolists. There
are supporters of pop art, for instance. And this
organized phenomenon isn't a representation.

PE But isn't it always a step in the direction of
representation?

AB It's a step in the direction of representation,
but it tries at the same time to be the opposite
of it, since it attempts to protect the immanent
exception by making it well known.

PE Is the content of organization different
from the content of representation?

AB The temptation will be to gain control of
public opinion, of the art world. If this becomes

the dominant factor, then the organization that was protecting the immanent exception will be in charge of a new academicism, the academicism of the future. There's no guaranteed strategy. Nevertheless, I think that organization, which I would distinguish from representation because an organization doesn't have to claim to be representative, can simply be the voluntary association of people who want to protect the immanent exception. I think this is what the schools are in the beginning, and in art they've always been useful. They weren't just there; they prevented something from being destroyed by academicism. They publicized the immanent exception and showed that it was universal, that there was something universal in it, that it wasn't just some particular madness. At some point, after about ten or twenty years, they became closed up; they became representations.

PE   But why, up to now, has it all ended up as representation?

AB   When it becomes representation it's simply because the explicitly creative period of things is over, which is only to be expected. I'm a Hegelian when it comes to this: everything that is born deserves to die, says Hegel. It's true: all things have an end. That doesn't stop the exception from being revived in a different form. Take the surrealist schools after World War II, for example. They were really a case of academicism; they were closed up. So this meant that surrealism as a creative period was over. But that didn't stop surrealism from being universal. If I read André Breton, if I read his *Nadja*, I participate, as we said before, in its universality. It's the surrealist *school* that no longer represents universality, that has lost it through representation. The distinctive feature of an immanent exception is that, as it has the form of a beginning, it can come back to life, it can be revived long after, beyond the representations. This is what I call reactivation, or resurrection. Incidentally, when I suggest returning to the word "communism," it's an attempt at resurrection. I'm well aware that Stalinism killed off communism, but I think it can come back to life. Likewise, I'm well aware that the surrealist schools of the 1950s killed off surrealism. But that doesn't stop me from being convinced that there will still be young people who will read surrealist works, identify with them, and create a neo-surrealism, and that that will survive throughout time. It's exactly like Greek art, which, although totally forgotten throughout the whole of the Middle Ages, reappeared during the Renaissance. It was truly a resurrection. And there's an even more fascinating resurrection, that of mathematics. Mathematics in the West – let's leave the Arabs aside; that's a more complicated story – disappeared with the Romans. Centuries went by during which nobody any longer understood texts like those of Archimedes. Nobody had any idea what they were all about. They were copied so as to be put in libraries.

PE   Without being understood?

AB   Without being understood. And it took the emergence of the new generation of mathematicians in the sixteenth century for Archimedes' text to be rediscovered with enthusiasm. *That's* a resurrection. Actually, I take from Christianity the idea that if something's true, it should be able to be born again. That's why I wrote about Saint Paul, after all.

PE Let's turn to something more banal. When it comes to the economy of the Eastern European countries, to common property, to state-owned property, do you have any ideas about ways to organize production? If we want to find solutions for the excesses of capitalism, how can property be organized?

AB The problem is twofold. Everyone can clearly see that, from a purely theoretical point of view, there are actually *three* different types of property, not two. There's private property; community, cooperative, or common property; and state property. The reason the second type has remained weak and overpowered is that the cooperatives are part of the capitalist system; they're controlled by capitalism in general. On the other hand, there were experiments in collective self-management, especially in Yugoslavia under socialism. This question needs to be given serious consideration. I think it's an even more open question in that, for there to be collective ownership, capitalist norms have to be abandoned. That's the hardest problem. I'll send you a text I wrote that's entitled "Communism and Terror." I think the big problem, which is also the problem that concerns me, is that it was a very bad thing for the socialist countries to engage in a competition with the capitalist world, because the idea that they had to catch up with capitalism at all costs, including for military reasons, became an obsession. Even in China there was the idea that they would catch up with England in five years.

PE   Instead of establishing new models.

AB   Exactly. Instead of focusing on establishing real collective ownership in their own countries. So, obviously, just as after the Paris Commune they'd thought the disciplined military model was imperative for winning, they thought authoritarian and coercive state property was imperative for catching up with the capitalists, because bureaucratized state industry was essentially the military model in industry. It wasn't really an economic model; it was a military model, and it was worthless.

PE   That's how it was with the Eastern European countries' economy after World War II: a military, but not socialist, economy.

AB   Military but not socialist. That shows how much the Party was about representation, not communism. I think the term "barracks socialism" is really right: it was basically general militarization, with all that implies. In peacetime, armies like those were an inert world. They were at once brutal and inert. That was my impression of the socialist countries: there was terrible violence and that violence was the other side of tremendous inefficiency. And they were unproductive.

PE   There was an absurd amount of waste in the East European countries.

AB   Unbelievable waste and false production statistics, because the military model is worthless in the economy. The military model was one under which people were forced to work. Under capitalism, there's an economic motivation: people have to work for wages. What is effective collective work that's neither solely wage earning nor solely coercion? The answer lies in people's experiences. We have to get people interested.

PE   Right, motivation has to replace coercion.

AB People need to be happy about doing something well.

PE We have experiences like that, even in our society, or we wouldn't be here talking about philosophy or social and political perspectives.

AB Exactly. We've got loads of examples, and we need to give serious thought to them. We need to put them together and see what can be made of them. We also have to take our model from somewhere other than politics – from mathematics, for example. I have many friends who are mathematicians. They're people who can spend entire nights talking about a problem, even if it's not something they're particularly interested in, and do so passionately. When they're done, they'll phone some other mathematician in China to tell them they've discovered an extraordinary model.

PE So we do have models in society. I'd say that this applies to philosophers who are not involved in academicism.

AB There are philosophers who aren't academic and mathematicians who are passionate about mathematics. As for painters, I'm intrigued by the fact that great painters are people who paint all day long. Take Picasso, for example, or Matisse.

PE Could we say that when someone manages to "work" that way they are lucky enough to experience the immanent exception?

AB In a way, that's the kind of experience that needs to be made generally available. It's perfectly possible to fire up workers' enthusiasm. I've known workers who were excited because they'd found a much better way of doing things. Workers should also be admired. Someone who knows how to repair a machine is someone very smart. And s/he's moreover very much in demand. There's one way of repairing a machine that's better than another way. But this needs to be acknowledged by society as a whole. Under socialism, there was a caricature of that sort of thing, because if you want to experience the immanent exception at close hand there's no doubt that you also need – and this is a dialectical point – for quality to take precedence over quantity. That's why the whole super-productive coalminer Stakhanov business was a sham. It was a sham because it was all about quantity. But quantity isn't the problem. On the contrary, the problem is how to extract more coal with less effort, less fatigue. Up till then, it was the worker who wore himself out the most, who worked nights, who mattered. Ensuring that quality prevails over quantity is really worthwhile for industrial labor.

PE   Would that be the germ of this new way of living?

AB   That's why it was also utterly wrong to engage in competition with capitalism, because it became a competition over quantity. People had to produce more, but capitalism got them to produce more with completely different methods: controlling the work rate, controlling each worker's productivity, and the fact that if a worker didn't finish his/her task s/he'd be fired.

PE   That's what was done to meet profit quotas.

AB   One can scarcely conceive of socialism as having the same quotas as capitalism. Yet, I think that in the socialist countries they did in fact have the same quotas as the capitalist countries, and, what's more, they were unable to meet them.

PE I'd like to go back to a very basic question. I wanted to ask you if you could consider substituting some other word or notion for the notion of communism, to avoid that association of ideas.

AB I've given a lot of thought to that, as you can imagine. Ultimately, I think it's better to revive the word than to abandon it. Intellectually, I think it's better to accept that the word was compromised as a result of a terrible experience, even though it originally sprang from a very admirable desire. That's what happened to the word. So just because of that do we have to throw it out? It's tempting, as I well understand, but I think it's a little like deserting the front and going elsewhere. It's better to acknowledge that that's what happened to the word. But all words, after all, have a sketchy history. Frankly, when Bush declared he was going to go to war in Iraq to establish democracy, "democracy" wasn't such a great word either. "Democracy" is a very worn-out word, too. In the end, what political word isn't worn-out? And even what ideological word isn't worn-out?

You could say that Christianity amounts to the Inquisition, but Christianity can be something very different. For example, when you look at the mobilization in 1937–8 of thousands of French workers who went to Spain to fight in the war there, say what you will, they were caught up in a wave of universal enthusiasm. So there was also that aspect in communism. Likewise, then, there was the Inquisition in Christianity, but there was also Saint Francis of Assisi. Hence, the word itself has ultimately endured the best and the worst. If you take another word, the same thing will necessarily happen to it, because – what I'm about to say is Hegelian – human experience is dialectical. It's contradictory, and so the better a word is, the more exposed it is to the worst. This also means that it will be seduced by the temptation of power. That's what History is like, and that's why I said that the tragedy of Christianity was Constantine, i.e., the moment when Christianity became a state religion.

PE   If it had been otherwise, would Christianity, too, have had that potential for immanent experience?

AB That was its original idea. It had that idea, most definitely. That's why I regard Saint Paul, or early Christianity, as a basic fact of human history. It's even of interest to *us*, because the fact that communism became a state commu-nism had consequences similar to those of an experience that was already familiar, namely that Christianity had become a state religion. When that happened, they tortured people to get them to convert. In fact, in the Inquisition there's the exact same stuff about self-criticism, the fact that you have to confess, that you have to accuse your-self of every sin. And then you're burned at the stake. And that's what the state, what power, is.

PE You can see that with Islam, too.

AB Of course. It's the same thing, but at any rate, if you read Christ's direct teaching, you can see that it's diametrically opposed to that. In Saint Paul, it's "render unto Caesar the things that are Caesar's," don't concern yourself with the state. Marx never imagined a Marxist state. It would have made no sense to him; he would have been very astonished.

PE Is there a sort of positive contamination, let's say, that spreads from the experience of the immanent exception in art to politics, to the family, to love? I have this feeling that there's a whole array, that the immanent exception can be found in every sphere, and that finding it in one sphere might make it possible to gain access to the immanent exception in other spheres.

AB I think it would. I'd say that philosophy or philosophy's vocation is in fact to take account as much as it possibly can of all the immanent exception experiences, or those, at any rate, of its own times. That's why I often refer to Plato, because in Plato it's absolutely clear that mathematics is isolated or identified as a possible immanent exception; that politics is, too; that love is definitely present in the transference, the *Symposium*, and so on; and that, as far as poetry is concerned, Plato is in an ongoing discussion with it, with concerns and criticisms but actually with constant fascination. When I decided to do a new translation of the *Republic*, I noticed that the text is filled with citations of poets. It's extraordinary. People are always talking about Plato's critique of the poets, but nobody ever mentions the fact that he refers to the poets absolutely all the time. What's more, he was one of the greatest prose stylists of the Greek language; he was also a writer. So I think that with Plato, as with others, there was effectively a sort of concern with identifying the immanent exception wherever it might appear. In personal life, becoming a subject in any sphere valorizes the status of subject and, insofar as it does so, the subject will probably be more open and receptive to the other possibilities that may be open to it. It could be said that to do philosophy is typically to attempt to be a scientist, an artist, a militant, and a lover.

PE That takes us back to the beginning of our discussion in the Semper Depot [21 March 2012] in Vienna on philosophy's potential.

AB But that's precisely what philosophy's potential is: to prepare people, whoever they may be, as much as possible to be open and receptive to experiences of subjectivation.

PE And now we have the categories to describe that process.

AB We've covered a lot of categories in the meantime. I'd like to say in passing that, for young people, I think, in this regard, that the simplest and most comprehensive book I've probably written is the first *Manifesto for Philosophy*, the one from 1989, because all the topics we're talking about here can be found in that rather clear little book, which was translated into German, albeit a long time ago.

PE There's a question that occurred to me during the era of state socialism. Many or almost all the intellectuals in the East European countries had supported and celebrated "actually existing socialism." I remember when I left East Germany and arrived in West Germany how shocked I was by the fact that the German Left, or almost all the German Left, had endorsed state socialism.

AB What years are we talking about?

PE 1973. Even Habermas did. How do you explain that?

AB Habermas changed his mind later.

PE Yes, but he supported that state socialism, which clearly wasn't socialism, for a very long time.

AB I've seen that sort of thing on a considerable scale. Just look at how many intellectuals were close to the Communist Party in France. I've never been. I think the explanation is fairly simple. The problem of the intellectuals in the West is their opposition to the Western regimes. Their specific problem is: what can be done about competitive capitalism? Basically, the key point is the idea that, elsewhere, there is a positive universality, especially if, historically, it goes back to the victory of the revolution. This fosters a binary vision of bad capitalism and, elsewhere, an effort that may not be extraordinary but is still preferable. I think that keeping your spirits up in an internal struggle by referring to an outside source is a very simple motivation. It's always been a very powerful resource.

PE But the idea of universality disappears.

AB No, it's above all the idea that universality is represented. That's part of the idea of representation: it's the idea of the "fatherland of socialism." It's pretty hard to hold on to a conviction without any representation at all, even though you have to try to do so. It's hard because people are always objecting that what you believe in doesn't exist. The objection is always: "It can't exist, and if doesn't exist, it's because it can't exist." This is something you can already find in Plato. At the end of Book 9 of the *Republic*, after Socrates has developed his notion of utopia, the young people say: "That's all very well and good, but it doesn't exist and it will never exist." And Socrates replies that it doesn't exist, but even though it doesn't exist *here*, it may exist somewhere else. Even he imagines that it must exist somewhere else, possibly. And I think masses of people, the intellectuals (and not just them: I've known very serious Communist workers, real militants, capable of sacrifice, capable of action) were convinced that Stalin was terrific. It's clear to me that they preferred to think so.

PE I think that that was a decision they made.

AB They preferred to think so, and, what's more, they could always reply that what was being said about him was capitalist propaganda. It took a very long time: the critique of actually existing socialism only began in the 1970s. It was actually very late in coming and began only a short time before actually existing socialism went bust.

PE I've always had an easier time understanding that position, in France, of defending actually existing socialism, because you were pretty far from the East European countries.

AB Right, the Germans were closer, but there were very particular consequences of the division of Germany, of the world war.

PE It was anti-fascism.

AB The German consciousness is a complicated one.

PE The anti-fascist argument played a significant role, even if it wasn't justified, even if there were a lot of fascists in the Communist Party.

AB Reformed fascists, right. There were loads of them, but they were able to make people practically everywhere believe that fascism existed in the West but no longer did so in the East, whereas many of them had joined the Party.

PE I wasn't aware of that either and only learned about it later on.

AB I know that, but that's the political power of fictions. And fictions play an important part in politics precisely because fiction is also a form of representation.

PE There's an issue we haven't touched on at all: the media and its role in politics.

AB Of course, there's the media. The media is propaganda, modern propaganda. I think the fact that people attribute enormous power to the media is greatly exaggerated. Take a French village in the seventeenth century. In the middle of the village there was a church where everyone congregated on Sundays, and what do you think the priest said? The old propaganda machine has been completely underestimated; it was huge. Traveling around France, I'm always amazed to see that in any little mountain village there's a gigantic church that everyone had to attend. It was like the socialist state.

PE So the power of today's media is presumably no greater than that of the old media?

AB It's no greater than that was. In fact, it's even more watered-down, because the media is more contradictory now, whereas back then it was a propaganda machine, and, at the end, people said: "Long live Our Lord, long live the King!" This is something I often point out because people are always saying that, in the final analysis, action is virtually impossible since the media is controlled by the capitalists. It's true that there's propaganda, a permanent propaganda machine, but that's always been the case. It was even a lot more the case, in my opinion, in monarchical societies. In fact, I always say that people in the West forget this when they say "Long live democracy!" without really knowing what they're talking about, exactly the way people used to shout "Long live the king!" in the fifteenth century, even very decent people. And every Sunday in church they prayed for "our good king," for France, for this or for that. The old-fashioned propaganda machines were very potent.